All Of A Sudden I'm The Bad Guy &
Parking For International Departures: Stay Left

ALL OF A SUDDEN I'M THE BAD GUY

&

PARKING FOR INTERNATIONAL DEPARTURES: STAY LEFT

Rants, ravings, thoughts, ideas and words.
JOHN E.L. TENNEY

Introduction and apology from the author

For as long as I am able to remember I have written down my thoughts. On the backs of the few remaining bits of elementary school papers which I possess are scribbled imaginings and juvenile jokes. For some reason I have always desired to remove my thoughts from their ever-crowded home in my brain and see them alive in the outside world. In the summer of 1984 I released my first self-published magazine called *The Slander.* This magazine was mostly the political ravings of a young suburbanite who was deeply immersed in the punk music scene of the day. *The Slander* was only the beginning of my fanzine/magazine obsession. Over the next few years I published at least one magazine a month and although some of them never had a print run of over fifty copies it was enough for me just to be able to physically hand my thoughts to a stranger.

In 1992 I published my first book of what I believed was "anti-poetry." It was called *"The Key of C"* and aside from being filled with typographical errors and spelling mistakes I felt as though, for the first time, I was giving people a real glimpse into my thoughts and my humanity. Unlike everything I had ever published before the contents dealt with love, death, anger, frustration and all other human emotions. Although I never intended to publish anything like it ever again, over time, I realized I would most likely return to my "anti-poetry" and was sure that in the future I would once more print something of the same nature.

In the summer of 1999 my apartment was overflowing with little scrapes of paper, gum wrappers and torn open cigarette packs which I often used to jot down my ideas.

As a historical researcher my files and data were in complete and logical order, but my personal thoughts were not. I decided all of that needed to change and so I took to task collecting together and eventually publishing a book which ended up being entitled, *All of a sudden I'm the Bad Guy.* I found as I compiled the notes and bits of ideas many were the same and so I also had to reform, picking and choosing, what words and word placements made the most sense. I discovered many cases where I had created words for certain situations or concepts for which there was not word. I left all of my self-created verbiage intact. *All of a Sudden I'm the Bad Guy* dealt mostly with love and love lost only briefly touching on subjects like employment or living conditions. Even reading them now I immediately remember who or what the situations had been that sparked the words. Perhaps that is why I wrote them down. Three years passed and again I published another book *"Parking for International Departures: Stay Left"* which again delved into my emotional states over a period of 36 months. It is, I feel, the most revealing of anything I have ever written.

Years swam by at an alarming rate and soon it was 2012. The world had massively changed including the ability to publish a book within days. I searched high and low for copies of any of my books, since most of the original writings had been destroyed, so that I might publish once and for all a final copy, for me. I did find copies of the books and some scraps of paper and again I set to the task of updating them into a manageable and readable format, which became this book you are holding. There is no electronic version of this book. I want to be held, pages turned, it's meant to be a physical book and a physical book it shall remain.

I can tell you nothing else about the history of these writings as I feel they speak for themselves. The brief original introductions are also included in this volume. I still hate poetry and feel that the words you'll find here are not poetry, they are just thoughts, ideas, and rantings. I cannot promise you insight or illumination of the soul, nothing so grandiose is meant by any of the words or combination of words. I doubt anyone will read this book, aside from myself and perhaps a few friends. This book is similar to having a billboard in my basement, I see it and get sick of seeing it, my friends only need to see it once.

So here they are once again, perhaps in their final incarnation. Once I hold the finished version in my hands and read through it will be slotted into a bookshelf and forgotten. Years from now my personal copy will probably be available at an estate sale in the box marked "All books 25 cents."

If I ever do write another book of thoughts and ideas, look back three lines and realize you've just learned the title of it.

Thanks,
John

ALL OF A SUDDEN I'M THE BAD GUY

A note to you

The following material was written over a period of seven years. During that time I was a small business owner, custodian, copy clerk, overnight stock boy, art director and an assistant manager at a bookstore just not at the same time. The majority of the writings are total garbage but I needed to get all the slips of paper off my floor and out of my head. I don't spell well and am terrible with punctuation but the majority of mistakes are not actually mistakes and are purposeful and, to me, make for a more enjoyable reading experience.
Good Luck,

John

These thoughts, ideas and musings are dedicated to the women and friends who they were written for and about. I'm sure they can figure out which pertain to each of them.

Closing

Pig's blanket
not keepin' me from swelling
with her blast furnace face
bullshop china
finding the way under
the floorboards easy
'cause it wants a new home
all
wormy and wet
mousey and nails
you ain't got the paint
or the ambition
to finds a new locale.

Smooth

mutter, mutter
thump, thump
am I a dog man?
or am I a granite hands
man?

F.P.I.S.

I hope you didn't take it the
wrong way
'cause Hoover Dam is that
exactly
and it's a big one
is it falling out of your mouth
or is the novocaine
making you a smokestack?
They come down man
and when they do
and do you will
and will is done
fire is coming down with it.
So, I hope it's coming out
the way I said
'cause Hoover may suck
or maybe
goddamn.

R.O.B.

That knowledge you bought
should of took the tome
named Thomas home
he'd be mewing like a bear
rug
or a crazy
crazy
cat.

Tuesday 2

night drops down
makes the concrete gummy
wet with visions
ain't catching the flowers
the way it did
but washing the bricks
can't be stopped
tracks are warm
still close by
far enough though
you see it

but is it ever gone.

Pocket

shell out a dollar for drink
and you drink
three dollars
and you don't drink
wednesday.

Later

You caught that twinkle?
what jar?
when noon?
I saw it sparkle
and laugh
'cause it makes
you think it ain't knows
it caught.

Follow

writing is free
cause people are reading
reading is boring
cause writing is free
you gotta catch the word
and tie it with string
but that only makes
for cartoons
you know?

Tangent

I did all right without knowing
somnambulist
don't make sense that
not knowing
means not known
you can skip around
a lake forever
and never slip on stones
when you do
if you might
you wind up with
trembling pencils
and clammy shoes
lake ain't a water-bed though
sleepin' isn't swimming
but it could be
if you got
pointy shoes
or mechanical pencils.

Noon

If I could stretch
as far as I want
I'd be all the way to
  a wake

Second

It's such a shame
that after
all these words
thoughts bulbs and birds
with the last
done first
the second
from
last
ends
up not
getting

done.

Spring

Take all that old
rigmarole and chuck it
down the stairs with
grandma.

Fresh

Chill a pie crust
'cause the apples are
warm
doesn't make good learnin'
if the cherries are cold

Life ain't pills
bury no good learnin'
round here
take a weak end
spin like a globe
now you're in Africa
don't slip your fingers

into the Atlantic
comprendes?

Thumb

I got the wobble table
honey
buzzing gets loud
and
getting sick of
honey
bees
but flakes crashing me
into someone's
honey.

18

Through her window
the world
is a postcard
beauty and form
known for romance.

Through his fingers
the world
is words
awkward and stumbling
but hopefilled
with chance.

**Mine is missing from this
list**

she
he
I
me
you
us
her
him
his

52900

I never thought I would
find you
it was just like
the dream
even the way
it ended

Untitled

I think
      and
goes in here somewhere
pointless
humdrum
monotone
annoying
and lazy

there it is.

Janitor

My job these days
is cleaning up the messes
other people have made
so
nothing new.

drop

If I kiss you now
I'd be gone.

tables

You said
write me a poem.
So I reached in my notebook
and handed it to you.

Untitled

And once where all had been
correct
and mighty
wallowing now
unemployed sunlight and
glass
showing itself
behind
where once
it had done the same
in front of you.
The way you place words
on the blank
it is amusing
i watch
and am waiting.

juney

I'll wait for the
water to
airdry
before I move on.
Who knows
maybe something
glorious
will happen.

Untitled

how many have you loved?
thought you loved?
knew you loved?
could love?

Number Four

while you were doing
the crossword
I wrote
dumb
on the placemat
and then drew an arrow at
myself

remodel

there is a door
that no one ever opens
but me
and
most of the day
I am in there
reading

An Ark Key

It's time to put
our feet down
well
that's what I heard.

the hour

did you ever pass notes in
school
i like you

Untitled

pound pound pound
they buildin' a bowling alley?
pound pound pound
or a supermarket?
pound pound pound
this has been going on
pound
for so
pound
long
pound pound pound
I hope
pound
they'd just pound
pound pound pound
stop pound
oh pound pound
the city pound pound pound
in pound
my head
pound
pound pound   pound.

yes

I woke up late in the afternoon
it was still snowing.
Standing in the street
out front of the house
I watched my breath
and discovered
I could hear the snow touching
the ground.

conthem

there was a house near
the middle of
my block
no one lived there
        a tree was growing
through the roof
When you stood on the porch
neighbors would yell at you
so,
  I went at night.

again

I spent an hour trying to say
you are beautiful
when I realized
I already had

thief

I found you today
but this time it means "got"
you can't know it
'cause it's just a picture.
For now though
that is fine, good,
more than I ever expected
but
my methods were as planned.

Isn't it so true?

my hands are rough

words

You are beautiful
I tried to write that once about
you
it didn't work.
from this
your eyes empty into mine
Where were you when I was
young
like you are now?
and I say now
like I am then

untitled

behind me
sits
with eyes
for glancing
at the clock
like you
which
behind me
sits.

see

everything is warm today
even
the sun

untitled

My neck and shoulders hurt so
badly
I can't sit right to write.

I'm exhausted

and she holds, me
          close and warm
her arms
          soft and
                    soft

plain

she is with him and has taken
her beauty as well
but here too
in my head
they are.
He should be smiling about
now
I know
I did.

unititled

still
in the darkness
your lips
found me

huh

seems to be cold
a yesterday ago
she'd climb ice cream stands
and moonstairs for
laying in his arms
both agazing at the luxury
of blacknight
warm times then
real warm
but now
she's ice cream
i's cream

r2

little faces
on a pipe
bearded crayons
used
broke bright
and paper
scattered
on floor
on ground
letters crumpled
sleeping
lounge
you read
laugh read
read laugh more
from love
and like
on ground
on floor

fables

she stares into the sky shielding her eyes
with the back of her hand/past the clouds
two black balloons are tossed against the
pale morning/as they disappear/could they
have been birds/her gaze falls onto the
grass/swaying until she is drowsy/closing
her eyes/trying to name the dark orange
color/so/he asks/are you mad/touching her
hair/she is sleeping

ripped

you got mittens and boots
when that guy
falls you see
        it's best not to help
if he don't see you looking
but just keep walking
he might not be
        ashamed of the
ice and legs
which combined
to fall him

untitled

The windshield is covered with snow
and the steering wheel
is cold
on my hands.
everytime
I exhale
you can see it

there are some things that you would
not build a monUment for
-I-

with two days behind me
I know I'm finished
-II-

I wake up in five minutes
I am beside you
-III-

my arms are shaking
you offer no apology

typical

untitled

it takes almost an hour
in the rain
to get to you
two
if it's not

M

I sat on the floor
looking at her face
counting her chest rise/fall
315-316-317
begging god

me me me

pulling the covers over her arm
the dog came in
I rubbed his ears
good boy
closing his eyes
head in my lap
I reached over and moved
her hair
from her face
and in the faint light
of midmorning

me me me

6ten

without direction
the days wound themselves
into each other
aching from the doingness
of nothing
drifting between hours
and bellyfulls
or borrowed foods

I don't even reget it

To regret the seeing of her face
          or even the wanting to see it
with the curl of hair that hangs down
her neck
and a smile while I try to
(ever cautiously)
(but noticeably)
catch her eyes.
And in the second between the second
where they meet
I see how unlearned I am
bowlcut with a stomach in knots.
Strange now, just now,
how I use to spend hours in my garage
pounding forks and nails into curious
liquid shapes.
Time is frightening diseased and slow
steering itself down paths where
I know there can be no road
I know.

untitled

at 6 a.m. I roll
into it
until 3
with 14 seconds left
I score

untitled

sitting next to her
smile
made me
the same

untitled

I hope you remember the time I said
someday when I'm old and sitting by
myself
I'll think about you
and smile.

untitled

there is something disconcerning
about her beauty
and I think it is because
I find it so perfect

untitled

if I bend this metal just right
it makes a fine seat
but still
steel
when chilled
is not mildly comfortable

exhaustion

I am tired to the point where
I am sick
my eyes aren't heavy I don't feel
sleepy or lazy
it's just
well
I thought I saw a giant spider
by the side of a building while
I was garbage picking
and right then
I knew I was
tired.

her observation

when I am upset
my eyes get darker

untitled

I stood at the counter waiting
you reached for a cup on the top shelf
I couldn't stop seeing your stomach.

untitled

Say it again
it feels good
very good.

track

my arm is around her barely
breathing her
shoes are underneath the top
blanket while
I
am under all of them
I
moved the television from the
other room
so she can watch it without
her glasses she cannot
she cannot...
I
am falling asleep

I am so tired I've fallen

and my stomach is full
fullfullfull
with headache and words
I want her
the way she wants
when the time is right
I will run into her arms
first though
I will have to find her

ad mire

I want to see you smile and know
you are happy.
I want to kiss your eyes again.

questions?

where did you think of that?
what?
where did you come up with that?
I just
it was in your lungs keeping you alive
and then it was in me
keeping me alive.

llaf

looking out the window
I watch leaves
play
swirl
and dance

circled 8

His hand
on the smooth of her shoulders
together
now
they fall

back to sleep.

half

Holding you close
is what I am made for.
Holding you.
I swear
I will do again.
This is my only religion.

last call

Will you miss me when you leave?
Or won't you leave?
Or won't you miss me?

circled 10

as water
runs over his shoulders and
stomach
she turns
facing him
eyes closed
touching
he pulls the curtain
from the wall
and the sound of water
is replaced by laughter

I think

he's been looking cold
she's been looking like him
passing winks
nods
smiles
it can take a good long while
to find your way out
if you're not looking

131

I walked into the night
blankminded
but not
just just
focused on so much
that if asked
I'd say
nothing
and it would seem the right answer.

them over

she pressed her
head against my face
my hand
resting near her hand
closer
closer

closer
finger
tips
touch
and our eyes are closed

untitled

does it seem
like I'm not giving out
enough information
or
too much?

rules are meant to be

looking at you
in my bed
smiling
I have to work soon
your smile
I stand and walk to the phone

circled 11

she pulls back the blinds
to see who could possibly be outside

no one

only a cereal box

on the window ledge

and some white stones
in the garden

arranged to spell

I love you

circled 13

The glow of the television
is the only thing on her

now.

Mapta

There are many
things I remember.
things that you
and I
wanted to do
Did you do them?
in the sky
are angels
and this is not so lovely

club

her breathing is beautiful
soft and softer
while I am seeming
not so wantable
or strong

good question, next

somewhere across the room
she is thinking

and I don't know of what

untitled

I have this idea that writers
at too lazy to write
poets are too tired to
poet
all these books and
open mic nights
those are for people
for and by people

Little scraps of paper that say
I love you
grocery bags filled with half torn
matchbook covers
those are poets
writers
lazy and scared
but beautiful
like night

untitled

Who is in my mirror
asking
who is in my mirror?
the unshaven face resembling my
own
only
he is old and defeated
I am young.

noon

It's so damned hot in this house.
i walk to the window and lift it
What good is that it's hot outside?
i stand in the sunlight and smile
Are you even listening are you?
my hand touches hers and they are hot
Say something.
talk to me
Please talk.
i smile at her
and I do.

untitled

I found a note on the floor
today.
It reads
No matter what happens
or why
I'll always love you.

Paris

Your presence diminishes the sun.

copied

And
looks down, sees me
across the sky
to the ground
And
has no eyes
I think
And
it's possible to know
what a strange gift I've lost
Closing my eyes
And
I am.

skin

rolling white eyes
behind
velvet like lids
I've kissed them
O
not enough.

untitled

how long can this keep?
prob'ly 'bout as
long as you need it
then
soon as you don't
done.

untitled

I've never
believed
anyone
anytime
anywhere
was perfect
except you.

untitled

not been sleepin well
hands are shaky
        mind is restless
feet ache
hands are
mind is
feet achebed
shak
rest
ach
bed
be
b

untitled

did you notice
for a moment
I was almost human

Paper gets ripped across corners

she said

your lips are trembling

I hid them with my sleeve

you make me nervous

she said

I'm sorry

I can smell her from here

can we talk

she said

I'm sorry

my nails bite into the palm of my hand

I love you

I said

she turns away and the shape of her hips is

It's hard to

I said

what she said

nothing

I said nothing

Wine is on sale here

She lay her blonde wrapped smile on my face. Skin
warm like my hands had been on her, lips the taste
of mine. She moved closer O god is it possible to
be closer? Her hands find my neck and I inhale as
much of the silence and night that can be held. The
faint THICK as she strokes my ear. How did we get
here with all of this lay and touch and closer? Is this
only here and now because I blame it all and for
allways. Blankets warming her skin, fluttering eyes,
all of she is asleep, words are slipping out of my
mouth my dreams widening out the windows it
cannot be allowed to stop. Never once would I tell
her all of this, unless, until she is sleeping. I've never
been that brave.
please
in the darkness
where my words are drifting
please
let her eyes be open.

sign

I felt like
I loved you
or
something good like that.

untitled

you would think that after
a certain amount of time
it could get easier
but
maybe
you
wouldn't think that

untitled

I'm a nice person to visit
but you wouldn't want to live me.

untitled

I need these days
like 8 or 3 books
waiting to get filled.
Ain't that much
word
in me
at least
not in my hands.

final

watch it
see where I'm going?
if you know
don't say
I ain't see'd it yet
those 'lectric lines
are hummin'
movin' the story 'long

untitled

I'd love to be kissing you
showing you
I understand
holding you
the way only I can
feeling secure
and cared for
even after I let
you
go

sumtimes

i gave her everything
she had already taken it
i wanted it back
she'd already lost it

Happy Switch

Don't birds live in Tallahassee
anymore?
They didn't come back from the
winter
this year.
Maybe, they realized
it was easier
to stay in Boise
and
watch television.

untitled

when I tap
it makes this ash jump

up

Which way is up?
more than likely
up.
But which way is up
up?

now

Do you want to hear it?

fine

you win.

stairs

that photo
of you with me
it's more than I need

untitled

I see it only took
two months
to put callouses
on you

untitled

it's loud
but to you
it's louder

little man with all the right chemisty

he sits in that
special room
smoking
but
he
has been
outta
cigarettes for
hours

fed

When you make me
bigger than I am
you've made me something I'm not.

How could you love that?

untitled

ink slowly
dis
sol
ving
into
my
han   d

I know

as I drive back home
just slowing for the stops
house by house
getting light
near the school
in the sky
is a bird flying hard into the wind

3

I have a photo of her in my wallet
she doesn't like it
I would rather be holding her

when I was leaving
she said
come back to me
and nothing more

outside of my window
is everything
right now
I can just slightly make out my reflection.

lines

The streetlights are filled with
snowflakes
and if I follow them up
they are
touching
the sky.

pass

she is
daisy
sparkles
starshines
but growin' in pastures
with slop buckets
that make
pigs no good for dinner

untitled

though I'm tired
I'm still
well armed
indians
and buffalo
i
can
c

untitled

my
town is
passing behind
me
in front of
me
she is there
with her apron
I cannot stop this train
anymore than
my
missing her
both are chiseled rock and
quiet frozen rivers

might

mixed up and four stories tall
I lean over my lifestyle
and make an
annoucement
"I am King"
if this were anywhere
and it wasn't
four and I wasn't fourteen
it might be true

rest

dark falls down
blankets
the light and makes
the air
a universe
I breath it in like
O
I never have.

answer

I called to say hello
but
it sounded like
something else.

untitled

If I could explain all the
thoughts I'm thinking
you'd hate me
more.

untitled

I remember when I
was so sure
I was right
and how
now I'm sure
I'm wrong
or was
or
will be.

untitled

it is hard
for me to
understand now
that everyone
wants you
or seems to
I understood when
I was with them
without you.

untitled

I've always wanted to be beautiful
for you
and when you say I am
I hate it
it means
some day
I'll brake
ugly and old
to you
with you
beautiful

untitled

one time happiness
came in
raindrops
each individual
but one
followed by
two pair of eyes

untitled

I would be on you.
Those were the words.
Do you think,
I wonder,
if I feel those ways?
Do you think,
I think,
I could be those words?
When could I say
I would be on you
to you?

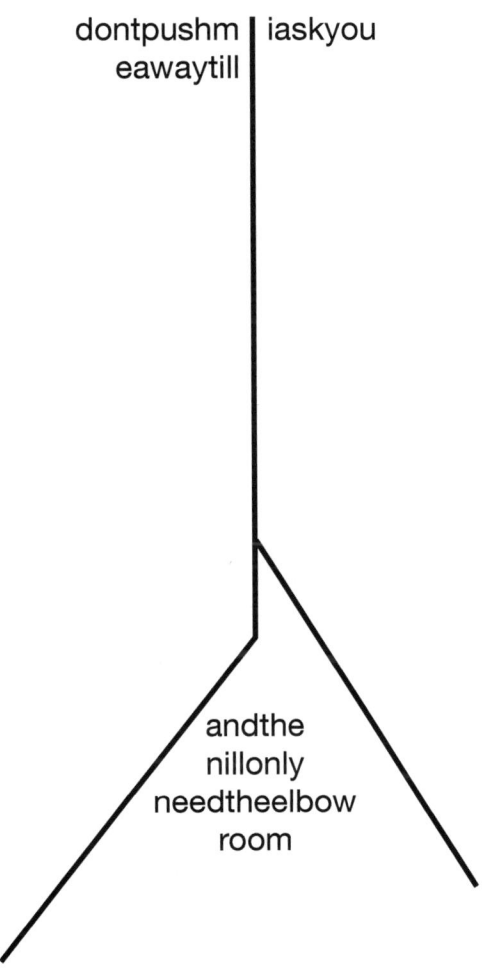

dontpushm | iaskyou
eawaytill

andthe
nillonly
needtheelbow
room

youar
erigh
tacro
ssfro
mmen
ow

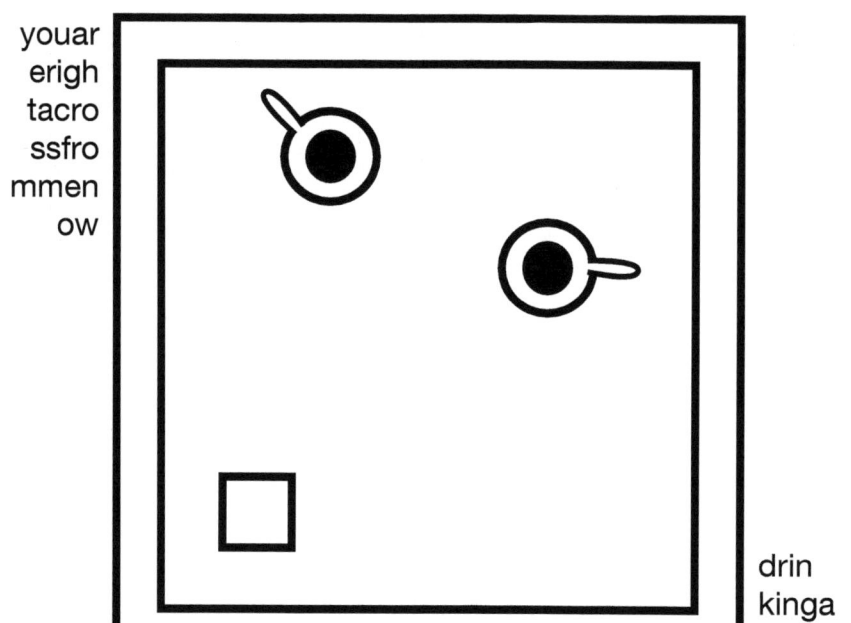

drin
kinga
ndcold

It is simply this and nothing more well it is more but it's summed up neatly in this next sentence.

I am tired and I miss your skin.

PARKING FOR INTERNATIONAL DEPARTURES:STAY LEFT

Introduction

The words and ideas contained in this collection began their lives during 2001. As startlingly as they began they also stopped.

John

9:15

When I realized
you were
leaving
I knew you
were
gone.

I hop

I can't tell you
why
because
someone said not to
but I
say it anyway.

The slip of paper in my wallet with your name on it.

With my arm
wrapped around her
waist
pressed against mine
she said
don't
but
this
was the dream
O God

this is the dream.

Hello Ceiling

I heard her say,
"I won't see you tonight"
she did.
I heard her say,
"I can't come in the morning"
she didn't.

turn off the television

Laying on the couch
your arms
around me
the fluttering
of your eyes
silent
moving lips
lying on the couch.

what are you doing here?

It was
nice
to kiss you again
that
last time.

No place to sit

They were calling
your name
searching
for you
they knew
you didn't want
to be left behind.
we are all so much alike.

dinosaurs, dragons, twins and fat fish

I held your hand
because I
wanted you to think
I was scared.
When you held mine

I was.

South of America, down the street.

Sitting across from me
talking to me
looking at me
laughing with me
I knew you were in love
with someone.

breakroom

My happiness
is hard found
quickly loved
and always
lost.

untitled

Everyone knows
no one knows
only I know though
there's nothing
to know.

wthigmt

7 hours later
your 6 hours away
tomorrow
it's farther.

Blinds

I close all of the windows
in the house
hoping
the words
laughter and
sound of us
would stay inside
it did
it has
it is.

unaffordable

I was
the best
you said.
Hearing you
touching me
I believed it.

cons tell a shun

Staring at the dark
clouds
moving
past
clouds
illuminated in
moonlight
a
single
star.

Where you are
there is

no time

laying in the grass
to look in

that

 direction.

someone is touching you now
someone is touching you
someone is touching
someone is
someone
some
so
me

lines through squares

Calendars are everywhere
the clocks
are on time
a second
lasts only a second
each and all is much too long.

I've been recently moved

Waiting
(as long as I have and will)
looks much to me like
my room
my bed
and the imprint
of your hands
on the pillow.

untitled

I couldn't imagine being happier

Now, I can't stop.

Survey

Of late
I have been
stopping
older men on the street
asking them about
their one
true love
each agrees with every other
she gets away.

After I hop

Sitting on a curb
laughing
close
this is so strange
weird
did you see that
        Did you see that?

50 gallons

That night
after you had gone
I stood until the water ran cold.

HimHeMeAndTheDream

Just when I was
finding you
I lost
who I was.

untitled

I thought about
you
        tonight
        again
                and agian

                and

                        again.

win place show

I have prayed
3
times
the day before
the night during
and the afternoon after

I should not be disappointed with
1/3.

E circled

Everyone drives your car
has your hair style
wears your perfume
it is not my imagination
it's my
punishment.

I cannot describe the feeling of your body.

42

I am not the
same
I am
real
I am
real
ly really
I am
real.

43

Everything is fine
except all of this.

weaks

The rooms are filled with
silverglass
mirrorly
re
fle
ctin
g

45

I was never built to hear you
sigh in my ear.
My arms in their design
fall correctly
to the sides of
my
waist.

46

I am stronger
than I thought
I thought
my undoing
could be done
by
myself.

August 4

On the calendar hanging in
the kitchen I've written

She will not come back

It was only a guess when I
wrote it.

48

There is a great
glory
us
inside me
imagine that
can you
imagine that
could you
imagine that
you'd have to
I imagine.

Scribble

Before we sleep
if you must have a
glass of
water
don't leave it
in the morning
by the side of the bed
where you slept.

1 Again

There are
26
birds
sitting on the phone lines
chirping.
I don't know what they're
saying
but I know
I'm not one of them.

Truth

How many times did I kiss
your shoulders when you
were sleeping?

210

2 Again

the shade of the house
hides
the blades of the grass
nearest our room
and even by one o'clock the
morning dew
still sparkles across the
greenness.

circled 3 bottom 3

Everything you never said
told me more.

untitled

When he tells you
I love you
it sounds different
doesn't it?
He's never told you that
though never told you that I
love you.
He says it meaning himself
but knowing it's me.

untitled

All those terrible people
          you've heard so much
about

well
I think they're talking about
us.

untitled

I'm sorry
I'm not.

untitled

My shoes are hidden beneath yellow and
green barstools.

Instant coffee sprinkled over vanilla ice
cream, in my bed.

Ashtrays filled and spilling on the floor of
your car.

The mirror in the bathroom reflecting a shape
of steam.

HEAR

```
M
y
n a
m e o
h u
a n
s d
a l
s i t s d                    r
k h h o                    b
e e a w              e
        o              r
        f              a
      you              t
                          h
```

ME

Jany ou Airy

Find my hands
upon you
my eyes

Find my voice
upon you
my lips

These
you search for
to release me.

To release me
you search for
these

my lips
upon you
find my voice

my eyes
upon you
find my hands.

4 Fables

There is lightning in this house
the color of your hair.

There are oceans in this house
the darkness of your voice.

Beyond the montain of pillows I
find the valley of your back.

The palms of your hand still the
words on my lips
in my chest.

We are all so perfect

We stand at the top of us.
Are we to choose one
at once?
So curious by design
perfect in our being
undone.

It must all be done

There is a particular way
that you smile
curving straight lines
part
circular.

Untitled

How lo
ng can you
hold
your breath?
60 seconds?

30

25

20

12

10

9

8

7

6

5

4

3

2

1

Woman stand front

In a handful of hours
I will place
my eyes
upon you
and it will be of no matter
which you
it is.

Elbows

I know you know
what a long distance
phone call tastes like.

untitled

Through the lights
of the parking lot
bats fill the black lit air
swooping
diving
and graceful as your hands
on my arms
hunting and feeding like
your eyes
never are.

untitled

beyond the forest
of my fingers
hides the light of your name
and the trees are whispers.

untitled

In the stillness
still
he is still.

untitled

I thought she was with you.

It sounds better than that

when it's meant in the right way

not spoken by the he she was
with.

untitled

Don't be beautiful
upon your return.
Be as I've forgotten.

untitled

There are many times
when I just want
to be here
with you   doing
        whatever it is
that we do.

okay thanks

Tonight I might
sit at home
not so much
lonely
        but
                alone
and it wasn't
until a few days ago
that it made any difference
until you
explained it.

untitled

Give me my
me
don't look

I'm all I've ever
had.

untitled

We can
talk
        about how we don't

or
we can sit here
and think about it.

untitled

my shoulders
are hunched over
breathing labored
eyes
closed
like first man
with first word.

village

it is night
with a black that eats
until black is ripping out your
eyes
and what is left
is whatever you hate in your
heart
buried down in your own
Hell
where
it continues to eat
perfection and illusion
which you
have come to believe.

untitled

Your hair struggles
in the wind
which is making it
more
attractive.

untitled

I have never written anything
which I would want to read
someone else write about.

About John E.L. Tenney

Mr. Tenney does not like reading or writing poetry. The thoughts contained in this book are subject to change and do not necessarily reflect the views and opinions of the author.

60271764R00048

Made in the USA
Lexington, KY
01 February 2017